PARABLES

FROM JESUS
BOOK 2

Deadra Neary

WestBow Press books may be ordered through booksellers or by contacting:

WestBow Press
A Division of Thomas Nelson & Zondervan
1663 Liberty Drive
Bloomington, IN 47403
www.westbowpress.com
844-714-3454

Illustrated by Bekah Jean

ISBN: 978-1-6642-9845-3 (sc)
ISBN: 978-1-6642-9847-7 (hc)
ISBN: 978-1-6642-9846-0 (e)

Library of Congress Control Number: 2023907645

Print information available on the last page.

WestBow Press rev. date: 05/02/2023

WESTBOW
PRESS®
A DIVISION OF THOMAS NELSON
& ZONDERVAN

DEDICATION

This book is dedicated to Jesus Christ, my Lord,
who gave me the inspiration and ability to write these poems.
Carolyn Williams and Great-niece Merrell Williams

Par – a – ble

A parable is a story Jesus told for me,
teaching me how my life should be.
God forgives us for things we do wrong.
He wants us to forgive others to get along.
Forgive the wrongs people do to you.
This will show God loves them too.
So read with me this story so true,
from Jesus, our Savior, to me and to you.

The Unforgiving Servant - Matthew 18:23-35

There once was a king who was very old.

He was owed by a servant, 10 bags of gold.

"Bring me my money, your debt you must pay,

or to jail you will go this very day."

"Be patient, O king," cried the man on his knees.

"I'll pay you back, please wait and see."

The king feeling sorrow, compassion, and grace,

forgave the debt as he looked in his face.

"Go home to your family and do not fret,

for I have forgiven your heavy debt."

The man headed home filled with joy and peace,

the king was good, let's have a feast.

Later, a friend the servant did see.

"Give me the coins that are coming to me."

"You owe me ten coins, so now you must pay,

or to jail you will go this very day."

"Be patient, young man," cried the friend on his knees.

"I'll pay you back, please wait and see."

The servant said, "No! I will not wait.

Give me my coins or your freedom I'll take!"

Others who saw, told the king who forgave,
"The man you let go, made another a slave."
"A slave," yelled the king, "This cannot be,
bring him to me. He cannot go free."

"The lesson, dear children, is to always forgive.
This is the way Jesus taught us to live."

Par – a – ble

A parable is a story Jesus told for me,

teaching me how life should be.

This we should do from the very start:

Study God's Word – keep it in our hearts.

God's Word will help us to grow big and strong,

with His Word in our hearts, we cannot go wrong.

So read with me these stories so true,

from Jesus, our Savior, to me and to you.

The Growth of a Seed

Matthew 13:1-23

A farmer went out to plant the ground.

He wanted a crop that was strong and sound.

He plowed the field and furrowed the soil,

hoping for a crop that equaled his toil.

14

He dropped some seeds along the path,
and the birds flew down and ate them fast.
Then some seeds fell into a rocky place,
the ground was too hard in this little space.
They had no root and they grew so fast.
The sun beat down and they did not last.
Other seeds fell among the thorns.
They did not last two foggy morns.
Still, some seeds fell on soil that was good,
Just look at the crop, look how it stood.

From this story, we have a great lesson,
that comes to us like manna from Heaven.
Listen to what this parable means.
It's about more than the planting of beans.
The seed is God's Word that teaches His way,
so we will be strong in our faith each day.

18

Because His Word in the path did fall,
No one understood what He meant at all.
So the devil came and picked up the seed,
and left God's children with such a need.
God's Word that fell on the rocky ground,
it did not last. It cannot be found.
You see it grew, but had no root.
It did not last to bear much fruit.
God's Word among the thrones did fall,
it was choked by the worries and did not stand tall.
God's Word that is understood and known,
will produce a crop given hundred times sown.
Plant God's Word way deep in your heart,
and from His love you'll never depart.

Par – a – ble

A parable is a story Jesus told for me,

teaching me how my life shall be.

This story shows we live in a world of sin.

By trusting God, we will always win.

When Jesus comes to call us home,

those who sinned will aimlessly roam.

So read with me this story so true,

from Jesus, our Savior, to me and to you.

The Wheat and the Weeds - Matthew 13:24-30

There was a farmer who planted some wheat.

His enemy came in while he was asleep.

Within the wheat they planted some weeds.

Oh, how bad was this terrible deed.

As the wheat grew and sprouted its heads,
the weeds came up and brought an awful dread.
"I planted good seed", the farmer said.
"So why did these weeds grow up instead?"
Don't pull out the weeds and I'll tell you why.
As the weeds come up, some wheat may die.
Let them both grow up together,
'cause in the end it will be better.
Let them stay until they are grown.
Then we'll separate what was sown.

24

The time has come to harvest the wheat,
so put in the barn what we shall eat.
Gather the weeds and they shall be burned,
for this is what the enemy earned.

Printed in the United States
by Baker & Taylor Publisher Services